EDDIE THOMPSON

# POETRY
*Semi-Skimmed*

⚜

*More verses about life*

with drawings by Peter Osborne

EDDIE THOMPSON

# POETRY
*Semi-Skimmed*

*More verses about life*

with drawings by Peter Osborne

MEREO
Cirencester

## Mereo Books

1A The Wool Market Dyer Street Cirencester Gloucestershire GL7 2PR

An imprint of Memoirs Publishing  www.mereobooks.com

**Poetry Semi-Skimmed: 978-1-86151-893-4**

First published in Great Britain in 2018
by Mereo Books, an imprint of Memoirs Publishing

Copyright ©2018

Eddie Thompson has asserted his Right under the Copyright Designs and Patents Act 1988 to be identified as the author of this work.

This book is a work of fiction and except in the case of historical fact any resemblance to actual persons living or dead is purely coincidental.

A CIP catalogue record for this book is available from the British Library.

This book is sold subject to the condition that it shall not by way of trade or otherwise be lent, resold, hired out or otherwise circulated without the publisher's prior consent in any form of binding or cover, other than that in which it is published and without a similar condition, including this condition being imposed on the subsequent purchaser.

The address for Memoirs Publishing Group Limited can be found at
www.memoirspublishing.com

The Memoirs Publishing Group Ltd Reg. No. 7834348

The Memoirs Publishing Group supports both The Forest Stewardship Council® (FSC®) and the PEFC® leading international forest-certification organisations. Our books carrying both the FSC label and the PEFC® and are printed on FSC®-certified paper. FSC® is the only forest-certification scheme supported by the leading environmental organisations including Greenpeace. Our paper procurement policy can be found at
www.memoirspublishing.com/environment

Cover design and artwork - Ray Lipscombe

Typeset in 11/15pt Bembo
by Wiltshire Associates Publisher Services Ltd. Printed and bound in Great Britain by Printondemand-Worldwide, Peterborough PE2 6XD

# CONTENTS

Short ones

Limericks

Six-liners

Long ones

Longer ones

"I'd rather encounter a weaker poem keenly felt
than a clever one that leaves me cold."[1]

Nichole Brown

---

1. In Kristen Roupenian reviewing 'The Kiss', Brian Turner Ed. TLS February 9th 2018.

This book is dedicated to the memory of my mother,
Mabel Parry Jones

Also by Eddie Thompson

Poetry Lite
Poetry Free Range
Poetry Decaffed

# ABOUT THE AUTHOR

Eddie Thompson is an expatriate Manxman who settled in Milton Keynes with Enid, his Welsh wife, and daughters Kirsty and Gill in 1981 (so not quite pioneers) after serving twenty-six years in the army.

After confidence boosting three-minute appearances in open mike sessions in 'Tongue in Chic' performances in Wolverton, hosted by Mark Niel, Milton Keynes' Poet Laureate, he decided to put his verses into print. He continues to quarry a rich seam.

He thanks Peter for once again giving his time and talent to marry up his delightful art work to the poems.

# INTRODUCTION

This is poetry plain, nothing grand,
Nothing serious, it's border-line bland,
It's easy listening, nothing severe,
Whatever it is, it's not hard on the ear,
What you get is what's on the tin,
It's semi-skimmed, it's pretty thin.

March '18

# SHORT ONES

These verses are short - Christmas cracker length,
And it may be said with confidence, brevity is their strength,
They're my observations of life, laced with a sprinkling of jollity,
And it may be said with confidence, they're Christmas cracker quality.

# SHORT ONES

Contents

Winter's Coming
Christmas in Guess Where
The Festive Season 2014
Cocoa 3
Paris, Peckham and Newport Pagnell
Time and Space
The Thomases
A Class Act
Having Fun with Physics
Our Afternoon Nap
A Rich or Poor Education?
To Be or Not to Be?
A Toast to Andy, Jenny and Family
What's it All About?
Rachel
Socking it to us
Alliteration
Celebrity
Hugs 3
Hanging On
I Think One's Out of Favour
For Learners of English
In the Black Country Museum
For Disturbing Dreams

# WINTER'S COMING

Winter's coming,
Look to your plumbing,
Don't forget, get it flagged,
Keep your pipes (and legs) well lagged.

# CHRISTMAS IN GUESS WHERE

Eat up honey, it's turkey roast and trifle,
And your Daddy's gone and bought you an automatic rifle.

# THE FESTIVE SEASON 2014

It was the second week in December,
And the festive season beckoned
Roll on I thought (how well I remember),
January the second.

Jan '15

## COCOA 3

So you're looking for a decent drink?
Yes, I know what you mean, nudge nudge, wink wink,
You have lost your libido, as we sometimes do,
Take heart my good friend, it's COCOA for you.

## PARIS, PECKHAM AND NEWPORT PAGNELL

Spied on the side of a yellow van,
Fired of course by a 'Del Boy' fan,[2]
Paris, Peckham and Newport Pagnell,
It really is a poetic creation,
Just look at that alliteration.

## TIME AND SPACE

Potter punts the ball wide,
Out to Powell, famed for his pace,
Who has eons of time and acres of space;
He is also, sadly, off-side.

## THE THOMASES

Dylan Thomas, Edward Thomas, RS Thomas,
Poets everyone,
What is it with these Thomases?
They sing a solemn song.

---

2 'Del Boy', a character in the popular TV sitcom, 'Only Fools and Horses'.

# A CLASS ACT

A woman I know has gone lah-de-dah,
For her the word yes, is now pronounced 'Yah'.


# HAVING FUN WITH PHYSICS

It gives enjoyment an added dimension,
A full pint of Guinness, with surface tension.


# OUR AFTERNOON NAP

Enid's enjoying her afternoon nap,
I've just come out of mine
It's one of the joys of ageing together,
The upside of a gentle decline.


# A RICH OR POOR EDUCATION?

Against your education
        you should hold an animosity,
If it failed to install in you
        a keen curiosity.

# TO BE OR NOT TO BE?

I don't know what it is to 'be',
I know that I am,
That's enough for me.

# A TOAST TO ANDY, JENNY AND FAMILY

May you always be in harmony, whatever your tune,
And to the key of E minor may you all be immune.

Jan '05

*On the birth of their second son.*

# WHAT'S IT ALL ABOUT?

To love and be loved, that's what it's all about
Alfie, if asked again, have that answer up your sleeve,
Look them in the eye and shout,
To love and be loved, that's what I believe.

# RACHEL

It was in the audiology department,
That to Rachel (alto and audiologist) my heart went
I could offer no resistance, as into my head she stole,
Then inwardly groaned as she told me, there's wax in my left ear 'ole.

# SOCKING IT TO US

Yes, we all have varied interests,
And different persuasions,
But there's a shop in Newport-Pagnell
Selling socks for all occasions. (?)


# ALLITERATION

Don't be averse when versifying
To a little alliteration,
It's an unwritten rule,
It's almost an obligation.


# CELEBRITY

When we were young, had we the temerity,
It would have been met with the utmost severity
From our parents and peers, who with brutal brevity,
Would have mocked a desire to become a celebrity.


# HUGS 3

The PC brigade we shouldn't appease,
A hug is a hug, not a sideways squeeze.

## HANGING ON

Before you start pointing the finger,
Yes, there are notes upon which I will linger,
Because when I catch a note that I know,
I'm extremely reluctant to let it go.

## I THINK ONE'S OUT OF FAVOUR

One wonders whether one is worthy of you,
But one's trying one's best, what more can one do?
*"All right, I'll tell you, brace yourself for the low-down,
You sound a perfect pillock, use the personal pronoun."*

## FOR LEARNERS OF ENGLISH

There are pitfalls with the word 'where'
Of which we're prone to be unaware
With the written word, this just will not wear,
So if I were you, I'd take heed, I'd beware.

## IN THE BLACK COUNTRY MUSEUM

And there they were, two anchors,
No – two anchors.

# FOR DISTURBING DREAMS

For disturbing dreams, try a late-night supper
Of goats' cheese on toast, with a camomile cuppa.

# LIMERICKS

A limerick, what fun,
I'm smiling already and I've just begun
They're not meant to say anything profound,
In the bardic realm, they'll never be crowned
So let's give them their day in the sun.

# LIMERICKS

Contents

Linda
The Erstwhile Speaker of Erse
The Bucket List
Don't Belittle the Limerick
Just Musing
Take Heed
A Rude Awakening
Rouen
I'll Have Some of This
Ironic or What?
I Will Not Go Gentle…
Noel's New Hip
This Spells Trouble
A Limerick with a Lithp
Ballakilpherick
Wiltshire
Hanging on a Branch
Eighty? So What?

# LINDA

A lady from Linford called Linda,
Baked cakes that were burnt to a cinder,
    She voiced the suggestion,
    That it helped her digestion,
As charcoal helped to de-wind her.

# THE ERSTWHILE SPEAKER OF ERSE

There was a young man who spoke only Erse,
Who believed the English language a curse,
    A renowned Gaelic scholar
    He would rant, rave and holler,
To encourage young learners in Erse to immerse.

# THE BUCKET LIST

The time has come, I really ought
To write a bucket list, I thought,
    But pretty soon my heart did sink,
    Of things to do I could not think
And now of time I'm running short.

# DON'T BELITTLE THE LIMERICK

About Limericks, what can I say?
To me it is poetry that has come out to play,
    They are shunned by some,
    But to others they're fun,
Like them or not, they are here to stay.


# JUST MUSING

Apparently, male poets need muses,
A woman who inspires, delights and enthuses,
    Who will waiver being paid,
    And accept being laid,
On Mediterranean cruises.


# TAKE HEED

Should you find yourself next to Mabel,
Keep both hands above the table
    If one rests on her knee,
    During biscuits and brie,
Your hand with a fork she'll disable.

# A RUDE AWAKENING

A terrific crash filled me with dread,
Fear of a sink-hole rapidly spread,
    But for ever after,
    I will hear the laughter -
Enid had fallen out of bed.

# ROUEN

Whenever you're mentioned I stifle a groan,
It's this share of guilt that I feel that I own,
    You were innocent, weren't you,
    Yet we tried you and burnt you,
Forgive us, forgive us — forgive us dear Joan.

His missus created a terrible scene,
Was Bonaparte tired or incredibly mean?
    How her nostrils flared
    When he boldly declared,
"Not tonight Josephine".

Look! A magnificent statue of Emperor Boney
Astride a horse, but something looks phoney,
    Bonaparte was five feet two,
    Yet it's perfectly proportioned, something's not true,
Of course! It's the horse! It's a Shetland pony.

                                Sept '11

*Whilst holidaying in Rouen, the group were asked
by the guide to write a relevant limerick.*

# I'LL HAVE SOME OF THIS

Does the advice "Cheer up" always go unheeded?
Do you think being glum, your progress has impeded?
    Are you always sad and blue?
    Then this course is meant for you,
'Happiness for Beginners', no experience needed.


# IRONIC OR WHAT?

My course 'Happiness for Beginners', due to start next Monday,
Won't, for the tutor, sadly, committed suicide last Sunday.


# I WILL NOT GO GENTLE...

Of course enthusiasms dim with age,
As if someone is slowly shutting the cage,
    But bugger this,
    Give us a kiss,
Then I'll break down the
door and with life re-engage.

# NOEL'S NEW HIP

The pain in Noel's hip is getting to be chronic,
Hopefully his new one will act as a tonic
    He'll tell Rosie, when worried,
    On their hikes, when they're hurried,
"Don't worry about me, I'm bionic."


# THIS SPELLS TROUBLE

Around the family I'm hearing a muttering
And now my dearest has taken up uttering
    I'm now quoting my spouse,
    "It's high time that this house
Underwent a serious decluttering."


# A LIMERICK WITH A LITHP

Many men are telling that they gave Beth a kith,
But they, I think, are lying, they are all wind and pith
    And they no doubt
    Did find out,
That Beth you do not meth with.

# BALLAKILPHERIC

Her interests lie in the esoteric,
Her chats with the dead are atmospheric
> She's a doctor of sorts,
> Reads palms, cures warts,
That's how they are in Ballakilpheric.


# WILTSHIRE

Wiltshire is full of phenomenal things,
Mounds, henges, mysterious rings,
> Crop-circles, defying reason,
> To call them a con is akin to high treason.
Wiltshire, where imagination take wings.


# HANGING ON A BRANCH

Those names and dates on a family tree
Like eighteen ten to ninety-three
> That's all there is to show,
> Worse, that's all we want to know
Of a life, when all lives are relevant to you and to me.

# EIGHTY? SO WHAT?

I'll be eighty next year; you're supposed to shout "Never!"
Not brush it aside with a dismissive "Whatever".
  Once, reaching eighty was something to crow about,
  Now, it's something you don't want to know about,
But you're right; it's not quite the peak of human endeavour.

2015

# SIX-LINERS

Reading these silly scribbles, you'd be forgiven if you think
That I've entered a second childhood, or well immersed in drink,
Of course it's poor poetry, completely without style,
But come on please, give me a break, I'm trying to raise a smile,
And now, because I'm ageing, my attention span has been cut,
That's why I like six-liners with just a suggestion of smut.

# SIX-LINERS

## Contents

ABABCC
The 1950s Remembered
Grace
Enough
It's So Hard to Do
MK Dons 2015-16
Go for it
It's the Cheese
To One in Need
Words Welling from Water
Alone in a Hotel Room
Hug Me
It's the Way that you Tell 'em
Gill's Sloe Gin
My Medical Anhedonia
Reshuffle the Pack Please
'Love is in the Air…'
Freudian Theory
Time's Up
On Offence
Jargon Misinterpreted
Mathematics
The Cuckoo
Great Shakes
Such is Life
Rhythm 2

Head up, Shoulders Back
Men, an Endangered Species
Ideal Marriage
From Dust to Dust
It Was the Drink your Honour
"Love is All"
How Odd
When We Were Young
Here We Go again
Melanie Reid
The Learning Curve
A Relationship Inverse
Nothingness
A Room With a View
Perkins' Mauve
The Referendum
Doc de Villiers
Honourable Members?
It's That Time of the Year
Five Nil
The Cerne Abbas Giant
We all Belong to Someone
Humour on High
'Hallelujah'
The Address
Peter Osborne
Vowels

# ABABCC

ababcc,
How would this sound in the key of C Major?
It would lack the charge of AC/DC,
On that I am prepared to wager
But strange though it may seem,
It is this verse's rhyme scheme.

# THE 1950S REMEMBERED

Of the early nineteen-fifties, what can you recall?
How about peeing our wages up against a wall?
So much to remember, how long have you got?
Some of it good, some best forgot,
And always the wireless, with Wembley football finals,
And always, always, those foul pub urinals.

# GRACE

I've yet to be asked to say a Grace,
But I keep this up my sleeve, in case,
> *"Dear Lord, if we eat until it hurts,*
> *Give us then our just desserts,*
> *And if we eat until we're sickly,*
> *Get us to a toilet, quickly."*

Amen

# ENOUGH

Today I'm feeling bitter (no change there then),
Why am I picking up litter
And dog-shit bags? Have I nothing better to do?
Well screw you.
After six years, today it ceases,
I will lie back and laugh as the litter increases.


# IT'S SO HARD TO DO

Ten years past my use-by date
I'm hanging up my hymn sheets,
I know I've left it rather late
As into my soul the thought just eats
An era is ending,
A mist is descending.

But hang on Ed, you know that you'll rue it,
Yes; one more concert, then I will do it.


# MK DONS 2015-16

To see the ball fly into the net
Is a sight to excite, not one to forget
But lately, sadly, it has lost its delight,
Something has happened to reverse the ball's flight.
It's distressing, depressing, how sad can it get?
For the ball flies too often into our net.

# GO FOR IT

Robert Herrick wisely wrote,
"Gather ye rosebuds while ye may"
I get the gist and it gets my vote,
It's carpe diem, seize the day,
Grasp the moment when your chance appears,
Act with courage, allay your fears.

# IT'S THE CHEESE

"Last night as I lay sleeping,
There came a dream so fair,"
We hugged each other warmly,
And we were both quite bare.
It's the cheese, the cheese, I'm sure it is the cheese,
Whatever it is, I'll have more of it please.

# TO ONE IN NEED

When the going gets really rough,
When you feel that you've had enough,
When from others you want to flee,
Keep in mind there's always me.
You may not find this reassuring,
But my love for you is all enduring.


# WORDS WELLING FROM WATER

Surely there can be no quibble
That from the 'River Ribble' has been drained the word 'dribble'
That the 'River Ouse',
Is the source of 'booze',
And that from the 'River Piddle',
Wells the word 'widdle'.


# ALONE IN A HOTEL ROOM

Alone in a hotel room,
Of boredom this is the height,
Without Enid, it's wall to wall gloom,
Thank God it's just for one night.
I'd sooner hear her snoring,
Than put up with this, it's so boring.

## HUG ME

Keep calm and hug me,
Don't alarm or bug me,
If all the rivers are running dry,
And the end of the world is apparently nigh,
Don't arm or drug me,
Keep calm and hug me.

## IT'S THE WAY THAT YOU TELL 'EM

What makes or breaks a verse
Is the way in which it is read,
For the nervous verse, the ultimate curse
Is to be read by a voice that is 'dead'
So perform the piece, dig deep into your reserves,
Energize your voice, give it what you think it deserves.

## GILL'S SLOE GIN

If your head is in a spin
'Cos you're taking it on the chin,
Or if immersed in serious sin
And face to face with the devil's grin
When you feel you will not win,
Swig a gill of Gill's sloe gin.

EDDIE THOMPSON

# MY MUSICAL ANHEDONIA

I've got musical anhedonia, it's a self-diagnosis,
Late onset, with a pessimistic prognosis
It isn't the end of the world, though my life is going to be grey
I will ask my doctor's opinion, but I can guess what he's going to say:
"Your musical diet is far too heavy, try something lighter instead,
Try Gershwin, The Beatles or Joplin, before going to bed."


# RESHUFFLE THE PACK, PLEASE

There are those who feel they've been dealt a bad hand,
That their life is a plot, deliberately planned
It's those high-value cards that they think they lack,
But the dealer always reshuffles the pack
So take heart, I beg you, things will change,
A good hand will come your life to rearrange.


# "LOVE IS IN THE AIR..."

There's a brand-new winner of the Romance Stakes,
A new location for romantic breaks
This will come as a shock, but strange tho' it may seem,
Venice no longer reigns supreme.
To the old Queen of Romance, this of course means,
She has been usurped by that wild young upstart, Milton Keynes.

*After reading an article (Daily Mail, 29.5.10) on romantic breaks, 'Venice or Milton Keynes*

# FREUDIAN THEORY

Tempting us always from one side is the principle of pleasure,
The result of a lengthy childhood of freedom, play and leisure
Reality stands on the other, the guardian of society,
The controlling voice of culture, good manners and propriety
According to Freudian theory, their conflict is the cause
Of our constant inner turmoil, and consequently wars.

# TIME'S UP

Singing the Liebeslieder Waltzes by Brahms
Sets off, around and within me, several alarms
I see them in the conductor's eyes
And hear them in my colleagues' sighs
So to quell these glaringly obvious qualms,
I won't be singing these waltzes by Brahms.

# ON OFFENCE

It's so easy to offend, and to be offended,
To have your equilibrium dramatically upended
Apologies are rare, for pride must be defended,
And often the offence is completely unintended
So surrender to the ego is not to be commended,
For as we sulk or seethe, relationships are ended.

# JARGON MISINTERPRETED

Holistic theories – theology
Laissez-faire – lingerie
Simple dichotomy – minor surgery
Cultural convention – college staff Happy Hour
Auto kinetics – pushing a car
Self present – a flash.


# MATHEMATICS

The Pythagorean comma, there's a name to play with,
Yes, maths is a subject that we really ought to stay with,
Have you heard of Braess' paradox, or Pascal's triangle?
Honestly they're interesting, your brain they will not mangle,
And then there's that old chestnut, the Bedford Level uproar,
Mathematics can be fun once you find out what its for.


# THE CUCKOO[3]

"O the cuckoo she's a pretty bird, she singeth as she flies,"
True, but I have to say, for sheer deceit, she really takes the prize
"She bringeth good tidings, she telleth no lies,"
Don't you believe it, keep the scales from your eyes,
She's the arch-deceiver of the feathered flock,
The only good one I have seen singeth in a cuckoo-clock.

---

[3] The Cuckoo, an English Folk-Song

# GREAT SHAKES

It behoves men to continually try
To keep their perilous attachments dry
So when the bladder's depleted,
Before the todger's secreted,
It should be shaken rigorously,
But not of course, *too* vigorously.


# SUCH IS LIFE

Could this be a mid-life crisis, early in my old age?
It's something I didn't expect, not at this late stage
"Keep calm and carry on"
Stuff that, that's a con,
It would serve me better to rant and rage,
To vent my spleen, to rattle my cage.


# RHYTHM 2

Poetry always needs to be heard,
But without rhythm it sounds absurd
A poem needs rhythm every time,
Rhythm's essential, more so than rhyme
Without rhythm a poem won't thrive,
It needs rhythm to bring it alive.

# HEAD UP, SHOULDERS BACK

You worry what others will think?
Well don't give it too much thought,
If you do your spirit will sink,
And in a trap you'll be caught.
We all have worries bigger than yours,
It's just that we keep them behind closed doors.


# MEN, AN ENDANGERED SPECIES[4]

The end of the world as we know it is nigh,
And it's down to the failing chromosome Y
There's no way to steer
Away from the fear
That men may have problems ahead,
Masculinity is dying; how long before it is dead?


# IDEAL MARRIAGE

Preparing for a car-boot sale, rummaging in the garage,
I dug out a book by Van de Velde called 'The Ideal Marriage',
First published in nineteen twenty-six, what then was the ideal?
What was the route to married bliss that the author would reveal?
"This should be good for a laugh", I said, stringing Enid along,
"Read it", she said with a smile, "And discover where you went wrong".

---

4  Gender Medicine by Marek Glezeman (2016)

# FROM DUST TO DUST

Some say I'm just a speck of dust
Drifting in infinite time and space
Well, they can say that, if they must,
But yet again, I'm told my place,
I am, they say, a bit of fluff,
And just right now, that's fair enough.

# IT WAS THE DRINK, YOUR HONOUR

"Darling, is that you?" Crikey I thought, that isn't my spouse,
"Darling", again; hell's teeth, I'm in the wrong house!
"Darling, one's on the tiger-skin."
Nothing ventured, I staggered in,
Discharged from hospital just last week,
This coming Tuesday, I face the beak.

# "LOVE IS ALL"

To be the only one in your world,
To solitary confinement mentally hurled,
To experience what it is to be lonely,
To be, you think, the one and only,
To think that no one cares a damn, to think that you're living apart,
To then discover that you are loved lifts an almost worn-out heart.

# HOW ODD

It's all very odd,
This belief in a God
For someone to say,
This is the way
The way to what?
Heaven? I think not.


# WHEN WE WERE YOUNG

It's on the tip of my tongue,
*Oh, what is?*
A pimple,
It's all down to Winnie Dalrymple,
Who bit it,
Once, when we were young.


# HERE WE GO AGAIN

In wars we're always involved,
You'd think that they could be resolved
By peaceful mediation,
But no, there has to be a conflagration.
So all join in this simple refrain,
Hey ho, we're at war again.

3rd Dec '15

# MELANIE REID[5]

The one column I will always read
Is 'Spinal Column' by Melanie Reid
Should her pen run dry, hearts will bleed,
Such are the works of Melanie Reid.
They're inspiring words by a broken reed,
That mirror the spirit of Melanie Reid.


# THE LEARNING CURVE

It's a steep, unending uphill climb,
At its easiest it's one in nine
We lean into the incline and firmly hold our nerve,
But we will never, ever, reach the top,
Only when dead are we free to stop,
It's a painful, lifelong toil, this endless learning curve.


# A RELATIONSHIP INVERSE

Definitions of the word 'inverse',
Include putting the word order in reverse
Turning things inside out, or upside down,
Like putting the adjective after the noun.
So, as to punning with words I am not averse,
The title seems appropriate, certainly not perverse.

---

[5] Journalist Melanie Reid fractured her spine in a horse riding accident and writes a column for the *The Times Saturday Magazine*.

# NOTHINGNESS

There's always something rather than nothing, but why?
Trying to follow existentialist thought leaves me high and dry
It's so obscure, I can't follow their gist,
They say that nothingness can't exist
But after wrestling with their writings, I'll be completely frank,
They are wrong – take my mind, it went completely blank.

# A ROOM WITH A VIEW

What must it be like to have a room with a view?
Overlooking a bay with ships sailing through,
Or a castle, an abbey, or a mountain ridge
A narrow-gauge railway or an old stone bridge
With a fence and a roof I'll have to make do,
But I really would like a room with a view.

# PERKINS' MAUVE

Purple, a colour that was once held to be royal,
But thanks to William Perkins and his mauveine
It can now be bought by those who toil.
It is worn by all and is everywhere seen.
On first hearing the name, it occurred to me,
That Perkins' Mauve was an STD.

# THE REFERENDUM

Nation-states are everywhere fragmenting,
Due to long-term tensions, over time fermenting
I sometimes, often, wonder whether
They are better off apart, than hanging on together,
Tomorrow our very own may splinter,
This would be for some a spring, for others a bitter winter.

Sept '14

# DOC DE VILLIERS

Hello? Hello? Hello?
It's our very own PCSO
To us, he's the long arm of the law,
Who against the dark side is waging a war
Hoovering fraudsters, thieves and muggers up,
Doing his best to bang the buggers up.

# HONOURABLE MEMBERS?

Milking the system, that's what it's called,
By Members of Parliament! The nation's appalled,
They're fiddling expenses left right and centre,
Irrespective of party, age, race or gender.
Expect a select committee to investigate the deceit,
And they'll recommend a pay rise to make the fraud complete.

April '09

# IT'S THAT TIME OF THE YEAR

Let's be honest, Enid dear,
It's a huge challenge to our marriage,
Any more than once a year,
And I'd be sleeping in the garage
I mean, putting up these Christmas decs,
Look at us, we're almost mental wrecks.

Dec '14

# FIVE NIL

Five nil
A bitter pill
To take with our gin and tonic
We'll dry our eyes
With our MCC ties,
Whilst the Aussies wax sardonic.

Jan '07

# THE CERNE ABBAS GIANT

The Cerne Abbas Giant has a todger ten feet long
It makes me feel inadequate, on seeing such a prong
But I fear he's under some stress,
Waiting so long for a giantess
His state of mind can never be placid,
As we never see his todger flaccid.

# WE ALL BELONG TO SOMEONE

We all belong to someone,
No one need feel totally alone
That's something we should dwell on,
When seeing someone in the twilight zone
We should bear in mind that their star once shone,
And that someone, somewhere, wants him, or her, home

# HUMOUR ON HIGH

Have you heard the latest rumour?
Jesus has a sense of humour
That's something that his father lacks,
And the Holy Ghost no wisecracks cracks
So, from Father, Son and Holy Ghost,
Jesus is the hoped-for host.

# 'HALLELUJAH'

This song, or hymn, I'm not sure which,
Is, I feel, emotionally rich,
It seems somehow to refresh the soul,
And for me it plays a calming role
Where many other songs have failed,
This my mental walls has scaled.

Aug '08
*'Hallelujah', By Leonard Cohen,*
*sung by k.d. lang and others.*

# THE ADDRESS

Just looking at the style of the writer's address,
You can guess the writer's age, well, more or less,
It's the slant to the right,
Used now by people of a certain age
In the top right-hand corner of a hand-written page,
With no postcode.

# PETER OSBORNE

Peter, you're hanging up your hymn sheets,
We will miss your talent and sense of fun,
This your career with Chorale completes,
Thank you, thank you, for all you have done
We will search the audience for you and Jill,
And hear your voice resounding still.

Oct '17

# VOWELS

A toast to that gallant little group of five,
Our vowels, may they and their diphthongs continue to thrive
Without them, where and what would our language be?
A series of grunts in a cave or a tree?
In English there are five, and Welsh has seven,
But Welsh is the language spoken in Heaven.

Dec '16

# LONG ONES

Yes, agreed, they lack content and style,
These scribbles possess neither grace nor guile,
They concern themselves with nothing serious,
There's nothing with gravitas, nothing imperious,
But you can't deny — I'm an inveterate tryer,
A ludic, frivolous, versifier.

# LONG ONES

## Contents

A Comparison

The Quest for our Holy Grail

Muse Required

The Corridor of Uncertainty

A Merry Christmas Everyone

Twelve Verses

The Tup

Ingrid

Emmeline Pankhurst's Mum

To Mary and Eryl, with
Apologies

Determination

Terms and Conditions

The Angle of the Dangle

On Being Human

Andy and Ruth

Anwen and Enid

The Invitation

The Civic Reception

The Civic Reception continued

My Container

An 'In-House' Conversation

Happiness as a Currency?

Unintended Consequences

Advice

What Can I Write about?

There's a Hen Pheasant in the
Front Garden

Fans Together

Dear Rosie and Noel

Trees

To Mary and John

Pipe-Major D C Hammond

Imaginative Descriptive Phrases

A Monumental Cock-up?

Spontaneous Combustion

Conniburrow Pond 3

Conniburrow Pond 7

Conniburrow Pond 8

Conniburrow Pond 9

Conniburrow Pond 10

Sensing Senility

End of Season Sickness
Noel Parsons and the Movember Movement
A.N. Other
Death or Glory
Milton Keynes As Fall-Back Joke
Miserabilism and the London Games
Free Will?
Mother's Day
Clearing Clutter
Fame
LBA
The Past as Visitor
'Problem' Undermined
Noel's Accident
People Palimpsest
Going for a Sonnet
Iambic Pentameter
Speech with Swing
The Autumnal Equinox
For Kev

# A COMPARISON

You perform your poems with a passion
Whilst mine I read standing still,
You dress in a somewhat Bohemian fashion
Whilst my dress suggests that I'm over the hill.

You wave your arms and move about,
You're animated, effervescing,
You involve the audience, get them to shout
Whilst in comparison, I'm convalescing.

I'm on a single shot, you're on automatic,
And your powerful poetry tumbles out
Compared with you I'm painfully static,
And my frivolous verses lack your clout.

But there we are, that's how it is,
In my own little way I'm rejoicing,
Though my rhyming couplets completely lack fizz,
It's my view of life that they're voicing.

May '10
*(After another enjoyable 'Tongue in Chic'*
*open mic session in Wolverton)*

# THE QUEST FOR OUR HOLY GRAIL

Myths, legends, folklore and fairy tales
Are all codes, laying mysterious trails
Most concern the search for treasure,
And are tailored to suit the listeners' pleasure,
The gold, silver and priceless jewels
Can only be accessed by winning duels
With monsters who the protagonist faces,
Guarding caves and other dark places.
These monsters are our wicked ways, cowering from the light,
The treasure our inner selves, untarnished, shining bright.

# THE CORRIDOR OF UNCERTAINTY

This corridor of uncertainty, where or what is it?
A deep philosophical essay by Jean-Paul Sartre?
If so, I think I'll miss it,
Or the flight path to Baghdad's International Airport?
Yes, that I could well believe,
Or certain well-known sections of the M1 motorway?
Answer please, and don't deceive,
*It's the uncertain batsman, trying to make his mind up,*
No way! This is a wind up,
*Just what to do with balls, that just off his off-stump are pitched,*
*Which works like a spell, as before too long, the batsman is bewitched.*

# MUSE REQUIRED

Muse required
For writer mired
On the verge of expiring
In need of reviving
Are you the one to light my fire?
Are you the one who will inspire?
Why delay?
Apply today,
PO Box number 33965
Free me, shine, fix my drive.

# A MERRY CHRISTMAS EVERYONE

All that bonhomie, of course enforced,
And by the retail trade endorsed,
But hey ho, it's the festive season,
And for conspicuous consumption we read there's a reason.

Psychologically speaking,
In the depths of winter, with depression peaking,
There is a need, with a taste quite pungent,
For an orgy of excess, to be self-indulgent.

And that's how the system works,
Consume, consume, or chaos lurks,
So drink up, get drunk, and be of good cheer,
Have a Merry Christmas and a Happy New Year.

EDDIE THOMPSON

# TWELVE VERSES[6]

averse

adverse

converse

diverse

obverse

perverse

reverse

traverse

transverse

universe

versatile

anniversary

# THE TUP

What exactly is a tup? That may well be asked by city folk,
Possibly with caution, as they'd think it a joke,
Well, it's a promiscuous ram, with the enviable ability,
(Enviable that is, to young rams, yet to prove their virility),
To impregnate an entire herd,
Awesome, maybe, could be the word,
The rest of the year he rests, building himself up,
To do the same next year, when the call goes out for a tup
To some that would have a certain appeal,
To me, it sounds like a pretty good deal.

---

4  Verse (Middle English vers, from Old English fers and Old French vers, from Latin versus "a turning of the plough", furrow, line, verse, from the past participle of vertere, to turn.)

Readers Digest Universal Dictionary (1986)

# INGRID

Yes, we all have a history,
But Ingrid had more than her share
Much of it remains a mystery,
She said so little of what, when or where.

Fascist, communist and capitalist regimes,
All three systems she'd lived under
Her story contained many untapped seams
Of events that would tear many souls asunder.

Independent to the last,
Ingrid died and took with her her past.

May '15

# EMMELINE PANKHURST'S MUM

Who was it that lit Emmeline Pankhurst's fuse?
From whom did she get her radical views?
For me it's clear; it could be no other
Than Sophia Jane Craine, her remarkable mother,
For Sophia Jane was of Manx descent,
Which would give her a fierce independent bent,
And Emmeline would no doubt have been told,
That the Isle of Man Government passed an Act quite bold
In eighteen-eighty one (it's an Act you can quote),
That gave every woman on the Island the vote.

# TO MARY AND ERYL, WITH APOLOGIES

Imagine how it feels to find
After being wined and dined
That one had left one's teeth behind.

They're in a mug, one must be blind,
And now one's brow is deeply lined
At one's disintegrating mind.

"They're old and worn and cannot grind,
But keep them if they fit," I whined.
"We'll post them on - you just unwind."

We laughed, they really are very kind.

*May 2000*

# DETERMINATION

There I was at sixty-five, with another boil to lance,
How to do things properly at the dreaded disco dance
Yes, I am a sad case, but at almost every wedding,
All through the big events, the disco I'd be dreading
So, determined, and perhaps a trifle over-bold,
For disco dancing classes on Tuesdays I enrolled.
In the class I noticed a total absence of men,
And also a total absence of anyone else over ten.

# TERMS AND CONDITIONS

If by certain thoughts you're enticed
Like getting married, getting spliced,
And you feel you've found the right one,
Act quickly or that one will be gone;
Should you succeed and marriage enter,
You'll no longer be your epicentre.
To give of your best, don't fail to try,
And terms and conditions, as ever, apply.


# THE ANGLE OF THE DANGLE

It is important, this angle of the dangle,
Said the tailor to the sailor,

Said the sailor to the tailor,
Would it jingle-jangle
If I hang a bell and wear a bangle?

Of course, said the tailor to the sailor,
And it's not for me to wrangle
If from your salty todger
You hang a brass triangle.

# ON BEING HUMAN

I have heard neither hint nor rumour
That Jesus had a sense of humour
As God's only begotten son
Did Jesus have a sense of fun?
Did Joseph, the joiner, Jesus's Dad,
Tell jokes to Jesus when he was a lad?
I like to think that whilst here on earth,
He enjoyed at least a modicum of mirth.

# ANDY AND RUTH

Between you and me, and this is the truth,
Whenever I see Andy and Ruth
I think of Norway; Icelandic sagas,
Sweden, Denmark, Carlsberg lagers

It's because they look Nordic, from northerly parts,
More like Narvik than Harpenden, Herts.
It's the Viking blood in their joint gene pool,
Going back to the days when they pillaged Goole.

With horny helmet in the prow of a longboat,
I see Andy Olafsson, berserker of note,
And handling the starboard with consummate skill,
Stands Ruth, with blonde pigtails and a cast-iron will.

Of their Norse appearance they're rightly proud,
And with such a heritage they can stand unbowed.
They returned last year to their ancestral home,
Where Norwegians met them, as two of their own.

July '05

# ANWEN AND ENID

As we drove into Northampton, Griff and I in the front, Enid and Anwen in the back, Enid broke off her conversation with Anwen and asked, "Where are we going now then?" I took a deep breath and announced, "To see the Church of the Holy Sepulchre, built in 1111 as an exact replica of the Holy Sepulchre in Jerusalem." That, I thought, must sound impressive; not however to Enid, who replied, "Could you drop us off at Debenhams then." I should have known better. To Enid and Anwen the Taj Mahal would be somewhere to visit if the shops were shut.

We dropped them off in the town centre and watched them walk off in the direction of the store, arm in arm, heads almost touching, an amalgam of arthritic hips and knees, conversing in Welsh, supporting each other physically and spiritually. They must possess a natural navigational aid with an in-built bias towards shops, which enables them to walk directly, even in unfamiliar surroundings, to a BHS, Debenhams, NEXT, John Lewis, or whatever, store. This remains one of the unexplained mysteries of human nature, especially knowing that unless they're going shopping, their navigational equipment will malfunction two hundred yards from their doorstep.

2000

# THE INVITATION

Enid, sit down, and take off that frown
Whilst I break out the Bristol Cream
I'm depending on you to tell me it's true,
To tell me this isn't a dream.
We're invited to sup with the Mayor.

Stress? Well now let me guess,
You've nothing suitable to wear,
You don't possess a cocktail dress,
Well you're going if you have to go bare.

I'll reply, we're delighted, and there's nothing up with your hair.
It's the lovely Mayor Morris, not the London Mayor Boris,
Who is hosting this civic reception.
Of course I am proud, but have inwardly vowed
To hide my pride from detection.
So Enid, prepare yourself, we'll be in the limelight's glare.

Feb '13

# THE CIVIC RECEPTION

Showered, shampooed and shaved,
Hair combed, ears and nose trimmed,
'The suit' dug out and trousers pressed,
Clean shirt, collar and tie,
Hole-free socks,
Shoes polished, soled and heeled,
Clean handkerchief and underwear,
I'm ready.
Oops – nearly forgot, hearing aid, with new battery.

Enid, who has had her hair done,
Is wearing her little blue number, with a stole,
And has just shouted down the stairs, "Nearly ready",
Which gives me time to read the paper.

Right, synchronize watches,
It's 1925hrs, 3, 2, 1, now.
Deep breaths, we're going in,
Enid, you go first.

*To be continued.*
March '13

# THE CIVIC RECEPTION *(continued)*

What an excellent and memorable evening,
It's 10:30 and we're home, elated but whacked,
The venue was the ballroom at Stadium MK,
Home of MK Dons,
Which was packed with literally hundreds of people,
Including more mayors that you could wave a stick at.
There we were joined by Simon and Liz,
The award winners had done/were doing
Amazing things for Milton Keynes.
The food and company were great,
What else is there?

I received my certificate and flowers on stage
From Mayor Catriona Morris
And Councillor Denise Brunning,
Chair of the Safer Neighbourhood Delivery Group
(Sounds like a gathering of local midwives).
I now imagine myself grabbing the mike
And making an emotional speech, BAFTA style,
Brushing away the tears with the back of my hand,
And with a breaking voice thanking
Simon Bates, Kevin Wilson and the staff of Great Linford
Parish Council
Without whose support this award would not have been
possible.
"I love you all!"

As I've said, it was an excellent and memorable evening.

March '13

# MY CONTAINER

My container is secured to a vehicle that runs
On a non-renewable fuel allowing
It to cover a distance of one hundred years,
Depending, that is, on how sensibly it is driven,
How well it is maintained
And on a huge slice of luck, called, by some, fate.

It holds parcels of cubic time,
Stacked in chronological order.
Each package is retrievable (so far) and unique to me.
The container seemed cavernous at first
And a feeling existed that it would never be filled.

But now, after passing the fifty-year milestone,
It fills all too quickly, with parcels of varying size
That contain a mix of positive and negative times.
To taste the essence of their contents
Each box has to be reopened and the nuances inhaled.

Every box affects its neighbour
Despite the padding that they're wrapped in.
The padding, of varying thicknesses,
Has an unpleasant, uncomfortable, aroma
It is a non-time, not a space to be in for long.

My container is almost three-quarters full now
And as the boxes keep coming,

It will be completely full in no time.
Then what, another container,
A more mysterious space and time,
Or darkness?

October '07<br>
*Based on a diary entry for October 1986*

# AN 'IN-HOUSE' CONVERSATION

Enthusiasms are hard to find,
They somehow seem to slip the mind
Once they came in thick and fast,
But sadly now, those days are past.
So here I sit contemplating,
My body and soul disintegrating.

*Well shake yourself, don't be so dozy,*
*Here in your gloom you're far too cosy,*
*You're in charge, there's no guiding light,*
*And don't blame age for your imagined plight.*
*Enthusiasms are there to be found,*
*So get off your backside and look around.*

Yes, OK, you're right of course,
From this stultifying stupor I must divorce
It's going to take an enormous push,
To eject this gloom like a toilet flush
But anything to stop drowning in sorrow.
Yes, you're right, I'll start… tomorrow.

June '10

# HAPPINESS AS A CURRENCY?

Have you noticed the move to measure happiness?
Is it a paradigm shift or new-age dappiness?
Of course it's something to be treasured,
But honestly, can it ever be measured?
Still, it will make a change from measuring the economy,
And the regular appeals to Brussels for economic autonomy.

If happiness can be measured then yes, it can be taxed,
So could it become a currency, when cash is finally axed?
Supposing we were paid in happiness, in all its varying degrees
(And assuming that the banks were down upon their knees)
If those degrees ranged from delight to euphoric,
I'd be in danger of becoming a workaholic.

But what to do with artificial happiness, that found in a pill?
Issued to the unemployed maybe, and to those who are over the hill?
I know this is science fiction, a futuristic dream,
But our current monetary system will one day run out of steam.
What then? How would we be for our efforts rewarded?
Contentment, fulfilment, happiness; maybe these could be awarded.

# UNINTENDED CONSEQUENCES

What seemed a good idea at the time
Will have unintended consequences, maybe years down the line
On a personal and global level, this observation is relevant,
For in making the decision, greed is often an element.
At the heart of every confrontation,
Conflict, conflagration,
Lies a decision, usually political,
Sometimes so old it's almost mythical.
"How could they have done that? It's an out and out crime."
But it seemed a good idea at the time.

# ADVICE

If you want to grab the reader's attention,
And then ensure their continued retention,
Expand the truth to near invention,
Bring them into an added dimension.

This may entail reprehension,
Not to mention strong contention,
Let this tension induce apprehension,
Stick to the rules, follow convention.

Would you believe it?
Would you Adam and Eve it?
Rules and tools, dos and clues, files on styles,
When my only aim is to raise some smiles.

# WHAT CAN I WRITE ABOUT?

*Well, you could write about what you see.*
What I see? What I see is litter.
*Then write about how you feel.*
How I feel? I feel bitter.
*So write about what you hear.*
What I hear causes me to worry.
*Then write about what you can smell.*
You mean all that ubiquitous curry?
*You can always write about what you can taste,*
No chance, my taste buds no longer function.
*Well you're either bored or lazy.*
You may be right; I am feeling a sense of compunction.

*Right, don't ask me again, I've run out of ideas.*
Hold on, I feel that my fears are about to disperse.
*What! What's brought on this rapid change?*
It's this very predicament, it's producing a verse.

EDDIE THOMPSON

# THERE'S A HEN PHEASANT IN THE FRONT GARDEN

Good Lord!
There's a hen pheasant in the front garden.
Pardon?
I thought you said
There's a hen pheasant in the front garden.
I did, there is, look.
Good Lord! Quick, get the book
You're right,
Look everybody, there's a hen pheasant in the front garden.

In an inner-city estate,
This is amazing, truly great.

Oh no! The ginger tom from next door
Of the hunter-killer class
With sharpened tooth and claw
Is stalking the bird, hugging the grass.

Well done! She's flown up into a tree,
And perches there in splendour, magnificent, and free.

April '15

# FANS TOGETHER

There is a Pakistani man,
An MK Dons football fan,
Who sits just in front of me,
East Wing, Aisle 6, Row V.
Goals he cheers
And refs he jeers
And sings along with the cowshed crowd,
Way out of tune, and very loud.

April '15


# DEAR ROSIE AND NOEL

The thing about Christmas that we like above all
Is the hugs from the Parsons in their front hall.
Not the Wesleyan parsons at the Methodists' meeting,
But Rosie and Noel at their Yuletide greeting.

Enid and I accept with delight,
The kind invitation to your party night
We look forward to hugs around twenty to nine,
But Noel – please – drier lips next time.

*Yours in anticipation,*
*En 'n' Ed*
Dec '03

# TREES

To you it may appear as a mundane, featureless place,
But to me it is my secret, sacred, spiritual space,
It's a mini redway roundabout, south of Linford Wood,
And I keep it clear of coke cans and other bits of crud
Nine trees of various makes stand around the junction,
That do, at least to me, suggest a Druidic function,
Three sycamores stand in close proximity,
These I regard as my personal Holy Trinity
With the horse-chestnuts I have a good rapport,
And I know what you're thinking — he MUST get out more.
I pass the time of day with them and offer up my thanks,
And pray that they don't end up as builders' scaffold planks.

# TO MARY AND JOHN

Mary and John, the Muirheads,
Both Aberdonian purebreds,
Entered the state of marital fray,
Sixty-five years ago today.
They've joined us here south of the border,
Along with their tapes of Harry Lauder.

Mary still possesses the essence of her youth
This isn't flattery; this is the truth.
For John she had a magnetic pull,
With Mary he knew his cup would be full.

John, when wearing his tam o' shanter, kilt and ginger jimmy-wig,
I 'see' him in his choochter shoes, dancing well, a Shetland jig.
He served in the Senior Service during the Second World War,
By the end of it he'd seen too much and was thankful to come ashore,
Escorting North Sea convoys, then torpedoed in the Med
Davy Jones' locker loomed, and he could have been left for dead.

Their wedded life together, as you would well expect,
Was, is and ever will be one that warrants respect.
Let's celebrate their years together,
Their ups and downs, highs and lows, peaks and troughs, whatever
Let's charge our glasses and be upstanding, I'm going to propose a toast,
Mary and John? Yes they're our friends, let that be our proud boast,

*To Mary and John.*

# PIPE-MAJOR D.C. HAMMOND

*Witnessed at the meeting of organ parts held in the church of St Mary and St Giles, Stony Stratford, 3am, Wednesday 11$^{th}$ June 2014. Chair; Pipe-Major D.C. Hammond.*

They're pulling out all the stops,
roared the large bore pipe-major,
(With one hundred and thirty-three years' service,
a definite old-stager)
It's good news all round
 we're going to be restored,
Bellows, blower, wind-trunk

none will be ignored,
We're going to make sounds to shake the building
 we're going to resonate,
Because we're the instrument of instruments
 key to church and state.
We're going to make sounds
 that would grace a coronation,
So let us all rejoice
 at this promised restoration.
Thus the pipe-major addressed the ranks
 with wind-chest wide open,
Of organ parts, which for over a century
 was a partnership unbroken,
But the 'C' pipe broke ranks
 sulked and stuck out its lower lip,
The pipe-major continued
 deciding to let it slip.
This isn't peddled propaganda
 it bellowed, now well pumped up,
This isn't just a pipe-dream
 it's going to happen once the cash is stumped up.

# IMAGINATIVE DESCRIPTIVE PHRASES

Stumped for alternatives for 'good' or 'satisfactory' when compiling staff appraisals? The following quotes, culled from the Culture supplement of The Sunday Times, January-March 2015, advertising films soon to appear in a cinema near you, may be of use.

**Film: 'A Most Violent Year'.**
Seductive and Ablaze with Threat. *(eg, Susan in Sales).*
Rigorous, Resourceful and as Smart as a Whip. *(Peter in IT).*
Fiercely Smart. *(Alan in Accounts).*

**Film: 'Foxcatcher'.**
Simmering, Pressure Cooker Intensity. *(Isobel in HR).*
Unique and Unforgettable. *(Pam, MD's secretary).*

**Film: 'Wild Tales'.**
Preposterous, Violent, Blackly Funny, an Absolute Cracker. *(Sue on Reception).*
Raucous and Wickedly Dark. *(Hilary in Marketing).*
An Insanely Fun Ride*(?)*
Delicious, Outrageous and Hilarious. *(Ethel in Print).*

**Film: 'The Face of an Angel'.**
A Sense of Mystery, Sex and Unanswered Questions. *(Mavis in Registry).*

# A MONUMENTAL COCK-UP?

We thought that the quote read, "From these stones arise and sing",
Yet the pillar[7] is inscribed, "From these stones horizons sing".
A monumental cock-up? No, the inscription is exact,
But the initial shock blew all my circuits, nothing was intact.

It highlights the dangers of the spoken word,
Of what is said and what is heard,
It brings to mind that old chestnut, once sent down the line,
Yes you've heard it before, but it *is* an old favourite of mine.

It left the front as "Send reinforcements, we're going to advance"
To arrive at HQ, "Send three and fourpence, we're going to a dance".

Nov '13

# SPONTANEOUS COMBUSTION[8]

Sixteen thousand fans showed their devotion,
On the day MK Dons gained their promotion,
It was as if they'd spontaneously combusted,
Like a volcano, as one they erupted,
The plug was blown, joy flowed unbounded
Amidst that delirium, how to stay grounded?
I stood and shed a tear or two
Had you been there, you would have done too.
It was a scene of unbridled emotion,
The unstoppable swell of a jubilant ocean.

May '15

---

7  St David's pillar, MK Rose, Campbell Park, Milton Keynes.

8  On MK Dons finishing the 2014-15 season in second place to Bristol City thus gaining promotion to the Championship League.

# CONNIBURROW POND (3)

Yes, this litter-picker's bitter
At the rich seam of litter
That abounds by Conniburrow Pond
A once calm oasis of which he was fond.
Most of this litter is linked to a crime
And the following examples accrued, in a very short span of time:

Purses and handbags (all empty), women chewing khat,
A torched mini-motorbike, crockery, none of it tat,
Five bras and an engine block,
Cash cards and an electric clock,
Drug users' equipment and an addict indulging his habit,
A full 'Power Force' tool box and an abandoned pet white rabbit,
Drug dealers and wheelers and everywhere beer cans,
All three benches nicked, taken away in tatty white vans
Empty vodka bottles, various cards, too many to list,
Bicycles in plenty – you're beginning to get the gist?
Twelve charity bags bulging with second-hand clothes,
Dumped bundles of newspapers, the list just grows and grows
Taken from an insecure letterbox, an unopened bundle of mail,
I'll stop here as it's a disheartening, soul-destroying tale.
Oh yes, the rabbit, with its nearby smashed-up hutch,
That really is the limit, that really is too much.

Sept '13

# CONNIBURROW POND (7)

It sits in our glass cupboard, in a conspicuous position,
Alongside 'family heirlooms', following tradition,
My gold cup, newly awarded,
And I like to think, loudly applauded
Hanging from its handles, ribbons red white and blue,
Its prominent position allowing visitors a view,
So caps off and give three cheers,
It's my first cup in seventy-eight years.
It wasn't a competition,
I'd just set myself a mission,
To keep the litter around Conniburrow Pond,
And just occasionally, a little beyond,
To a level acceptable,
Sort of respectable.
So, to the committee of our 'Big Local',
And here I become unusually vocal,
Thank you for your thank you, the certificate and cup,
Should I ever feel downhearted, they will lift me up.

Feb '15

# CONNIBURROW POND (8)

I met her, just once, down by Conniburrow Pond,
Thirtyish, attractive, smartly dressed and blonde
Lydia from Slovakia, (Bratislava, just a touch beyond),
Who with her affectionate dog had an obvious bond.

But had I seen an apparition, had my mind been conned?
Had I overdosed on Vick, had someone waved a wand?
Should I have the pleasure again, how would I respond?
I'd probably give her dog-poo bags down by Conniburrow Pond.

Feb '15

# CONNIBURROW POND (9)

Failing a word to the police from a grass,
I'd stake out the pond with a troop from the SAS
He's got to be arrested,
His motive probed, his sanity tested,
For it's now the fourth time
He's committed this crime.

He has a problem, no doubt about it,
(It could be a she, but I very much doubt it),
It has now become a personal matter,
I want the felon's head on a platter.
It's the mutilation, above and beyond,
Of the brand-new benches by Conniburrow Pond.

Feb '15

# CONNIBURROW POND (10)

It's a very mild mid-March morning,
And in Conniburrow Pond the frogs are spawning,
They've gathered here for what looks like a bonk-fest,
And they're going at it with an unbridled zest.
This annual event to frogs must be stirring,
Their chorus resembles a happy cat purring.
It's a marvel, given the stress the pond is under,
To witness here such a wildlife wonder.

March '15

# SENSING SENILITY

How can I put this? How can I voice my fear?
Perhaps another question will help to make it clear
Is the descent to senility a gentle but slippery slope?
Or is it a dramatic fall, without ice-pick, snap-ring or rope?
If it's the former, then I'm on it for sure,
For the smell is in my nostrils, it's the smell of a putrid sewer.

The symptoms are there for all to see,
They're blatantly obvious, even to me,
And I understand now why some of the old
Choose to sit and say nowt, like sheep in the fold
It dodges the comment, "Listen to the fool",
It's the easy option, avoiding ridicule.

# END OF SEASON SICKNESS

The football season is drawing to a disappointing close,
Another tale of almost, nearly, of high spots and of lows,
Those early expectations now seem overrated,
Those short hopes and aims now sadly deflated.
We're neither in the drop-zone, nor in the hunt for promotion,
We're roughly in the middle, becalmed in an otherwise stormy ocean
For what might have been but wasn't we're yet again kept waiting,
And for players, club and fans, this is achingly frustrating.
But that's how it is; we'll be here again when next season starts,
Cheering them on 'till our voices have gone, and willing them on with our hearts.

April '13

# SPEECH WITH SWING

Certain phrases possess a beat,
To the musically minded they're rhythmically neat
Personal perusal,
Erotic arousal,
Regretful refusal,
Etcetera etcetera.
There really is a plethora,
Say them with feeling and you've almost got a tune
And of course to wordsmiths they are a definite boon,
But however often I roll them off my tongue,
Their poetic use defeats me, they remain a song unsung.

EDDIE THOMPSON

# THE AUTUMNAL EQUINOX

The autumnal equinox, so I hear,
Is the point in Virgo on the celestial sphere
At which the celestial equator and the ecliptic intersect,
I just can't grasp that, so, do I have a stunted intellect?

Anyway, whatever, they say it has the power to disrupt,
It disturbs the course of human affairs and the changes can be abrupt,
It's with us today, the twenty-second, and I've lost my keys,
Broken my glasses and suffered a harrowing hernia squeeze.

It's enough to make a doubter believe
In this astrology stuff, as I mope and grieve,
But there's a convenient upside to these three shocks,
It's not that I'm stupid, it's the equinox.

# NOEL PARSONS AND THE MOVEMBER MOVEMENT

Noel has joined the Movember Movement,
He's growing a 'tash as a facial improvement
No, I'm joking, it isn't really a handsome enhancer,
It's to draw attention to prostate cancer.

Its full potential may take some years,
As it's trained to meet the hairs from his ears
It's thin right now but who knows, as it grows
It may thicken up with the hairs from his nose.

There's a menu of styles from which he can choose,
A veritable catalogue which he can peruse
Victorian military, waxed groomed but prickly,
Or Royal Air Force handlebar, full flowing but tickly.

It's due to come off at the end of November,
Whether or not, it's a sight to remember.

# A. N. OTHER

Amongst the many others,
There are those who lift you up
Whilst others, on the other hand,
Put poison in your cup
From that vile purveyor of venom,
We have to blow their cover
From that most ubiquitous slanderer,
That mysterious, malignant, A. N. Other.

# DEATH OR GLORY

I'm not one to practise deception,
But if an altered state of perception
Is what you seek on New Year's Eve
(Keeping in mind that I don't deceive)
Then imbibe a pint of the Tring Brewery beer
Death or Glory, to put you in a different sphere.[9]

---

9 After being introduced to it by Noel in 'The Lamb' in Stoke Goldington.

But be warned, at 7.2 it isn't weak,
It could blow your socks off, so to speak.

For the Queen's Royal Lancers it's especially brewed,
It fuels the panache with which they're endued
And it's given in buckets to the officers' horses
Before they sail over steeplechase courses.

So, to reach your inner self, and set it off in motion,
I recommend this nectar, this cavalryman's potion.

# MILTON KEYNES AS FALL-BACK JOKE

To all you would-be comedians who are having a go at MK,
Your tired old jokes are wearing thin
Yet still they'll get you a laugh, as ridicule earns your pay.

That laugh will inflate your ego, which must be fairly flat,
It'll help you to feel superior,
It's the comedian's equivalent of kicking the cat.

Hence Irish jokes, Jewish jokes and Polish jokes in Russian,
They deflect your own shortcomings,
They're your metaphorical cushion.

I'm sure that you think you're incredibly witty,
But you're not, you're being sarcastic,
Come, stay with us for a week, we'll show you an amazing city.

## MISERABILISM AND THE LONDON OLYMPICS

What is a militant miserabilist?
No, not a militant Islamist,
Are we subscribing to miserabilism?
NO, NO, NO, not Liberalism,
It's this word 'miserabilism', met with just last week,
It's now in the language that journalists speak.
I may be spelling it incorrectly,
As I'm approaching the word indirectly.

Is it an ideology of the mean and cynical?
Possibly; or of pessimism the ultimate pinnacle?
Amongst the depressed, is it an elitism?
Much, much, lower than downright defeatism
Or is it the creed of the nay-sayers?
Camp followers of the joy-slayers.
Whatever it is, or was, it's been banished,
Thanks to the Games, it has virtually vanished.

Aug '12

## FREE WILL?

"Just be yourself." Well yes, but what exactly does that mean?
Am I an amalgam of DNA, from ancestors long dead
that determine my every action? Then I am but a sheen.
Or is a divine source determining the paths I tread?

Or am I acting ascribed roles, a kind of social build?
Or simply doing nothing but conforming to the crowd?
If any of these are true, can I really be free-willed?
Can I be autonomous, and live my life unbowed?

You worry too much, I know, it's in my genes,
Rubbish! Stop asking yourself what everything means,
Just be yourself, don't act, be natural,
Like the song says, "Everything is satisfactual".

# MOTHERS' DAY

Today is Mothers' Day,
And reading of others' mothers, my thoughts turn to my own.
What a sad time she had of it,
Things should have been so different for her.
It's as well that what lay ahead of her remained unknown
She deserved better.

Made to live a lie, that's the saddest part,
Born out of wedlock, a sin to the bigoted,
Born and bred in rural North Wales,
Letters describe her setting off to Sunday school, cheerful and smart.

Abandoned by her husband,
She died of cancer more than half a century past,
Before she could see her son married, or her granddaughters,
Before I could say good-bye
She deserved better, her life, I feel, had been tragically miscast.

What a lovely woman she was,
Attractive when young, with a loving nature and sense of humour
That endeared her to her friends
Her tears I can readily recall,
Caused by her plight and that bloody tumour.
She deserved better.

March '10

# CLEARING CLUTTER

What once brought us bread and butter
Is now regarded as useless clutter
The time has come that I've always feared,
When all this clutter has got to be cleared
Shelves and boxes, bursting with 'stuff',
Now worthless, unwanted; but it's going to be tough
So, with a despondent, heavy heart,
Tomorrow I'm going to make a start.
But away with fear and trepidation,
It is after all, just, preparation.

# FAME

The MK Dons and Crawley match was rapidly looming,
At the city-centre kiosk ticket sales were booming
And when buying my ticket, making the transaction,
Up went the cry, "Lights, camera, action!"
There was no time for make-up, nor to go over my line,

No wait in the 'green room' with a glass of fortified wine
The clip went out that evening, on the BBC's 'Look East',
My fifteen seconds of fame, of vanity a feast
It's a BAFTA nomination for the lady at the stall,
Her acting was flawless; she deserved a curtain call
And I have been informed, by a media mole,
That I am also up, for the 'Best Supporting Role'.

Sept '14

## LBA

Come litter-bugs, be one of us,
We're Litter Bugs Anonymous
We'll help you to ditch your addiction,
We'll help you to lick your affliction,
To break the habit, to litter no more,
On this landscape of litter, to wage a war.
Together we can end this national shame,
And our mislaid civic pride reclaim.

## THE PAST AS VISITOR

You will have noticed that our past never leaves us,
Which is fair enough;
After all, it has made us what we are.
People and events cling to our memory banks,
But we know that memory plays tricks on us,
Fifty, sixty years ago can appear as yesterday,

Whilst yesterday remains hidden in dead ground.
As if to confirm that events did actually happen
People surface, out of the blue,
People who shared your experiences, good and bad.

Take yesterday, whilst waiting my turn at the barber's,
I picked up the *Daily Mirror*,
And there he was, on page 27,
Forty years on, Ralph Bagnall-Wild,
Servicing his model railway in his back garden.
My boss in the army during the period 1971-74
When based at Lulworth Dorset,
Alive and well and living near Whitby,
In the barber's chair I downloaded memories of that period
The past can be a welcome visitor.

# 'PROBLEM' UNDERMINED

Have you noticed the word 'problem' is no longer used?
It has been neutered, sterilized, deadened, defused
Problems are now 'issues', weakened by a word
Which blunts the truthful 'problem', now seriously blurred
Or else it is a 'challenge' which invites you in,
"Do you like a challenge?" It's a game that you might win.
So is 'problem' soon to be seen as outdated,
Destined for the dustbin, archaic and antiquated?

# NOEL'S ACCIDENT

It's another tale of the completely unexpected,
A warning to us all of a danger oft neglected,
It's those not to be taken lightly risk-full 'apples and pears',
That deadly dangerous, sometimes fatal, in-house flight of stairs.
Well our good friend Noel down his stairs cascaded,
Spectacular is the word, and completely unaided,
His sixteen stone (a guess), landed on both knees,
Severing the tendons, to mobility the keys,
Can you feel the pain? Can you hear the tear?
It must have been horrendous, more than I could bear
Noel is an outdoor man and, with Rosie, a hiking fanatic,
For six months, they say, he'll be grounded, boringly static
So how will he with this forced inertia grapple?
It will, they also say, stop him farting in chapel.


# PEOPLE PALIMPSEST

As we're 'worked on' many times, are we not each a palimpsest?
A lifetime of differing roles (each putting us to the test),
Each bringing its mask, which to our face becomes cemented,
So the original is suffocated, buried unlamented.
Each mask demands an act, which, of course, involves deception,
At which we become so adept it almost defies detection.
A lengthy course of restoration is going to be required,
To reveal the original you, should that be desired
So, as we're under many layers (at society's behest),
There may be a case for thinking that we're all a palimpsest.

# GOING FOR A SONNET

These poems of yours are getting shorter,
Commented Gill, our youngest daughter
Whatever happened to the old six-liner?
'Right!' I said, my old China,
'I'll do my best to make them longer,
Longer than your normal conga
I hope you've noticed, unless I'm wrong,
This one's already eight lines long.
Forget the quality, feel the length,
And anyway, quality is not my strength
So, my cherub, hold on to your bonnet,
As you can see, I'm going for a sonnet
A sonnet of sorts, at least in one sense,
Even though it's utter nonsense.'

# IAMBIC PENTAMETER

It's all about metre, rhythm and stress,
If used correctly, it does add finesse

But when I try to stick to the rules,
My ardour to use it definitely cools.

Trochees and spondees, and then pyrrhic feet
Enjambments and end stops, my mind unseat.

I won't give it up mind, Stephen Fry[10] is right,
Heroic verse will come one day; well, it might.

---

10  Stephen Fry (2005) 'The Ode Less Travelled' Hutchinson

# FOR KEV

On a Conniburrow roundabout there's a sacred shrine

For Kev; a mass of flowers and flags and Fosters, and a few bottles of wine

On the evening of his murder sixty people gathered there,

For Kev; to sing and drink to his memory and to say a sort of prayer,

The police arrived, not knowing that they were mourning

For Kev; the police moved on, the mourners stayed to see a new day dawning.

Friends take it in turns to sit through the night with the flowers placed

For Kev; and ponder on their loss, on the tragic, futile waste,

It's by the corner shops, this colourful, moving reverence

For Kev; for family and friends it may ease their painful severance,

I never knew him — more's the pity — but I want to add my little bit,

> For Kev.
> September '07

# LONGER ONES

Your hopes of finding quality I beg you now discard,
For in this genre "Longer Ones", it's poetry by the yard.

# LONGER ONES

Contents

The Papers
Map Reading
The Famous Five Ring Their Red Kite
Lancia

# THE PAPERS

It's a sort of praise poem for the British press,
Though the rhythm and metre may end in a mess.

Local and national, they all wave their flag,
And range from the brilliant to the fish and chip rag.

Sensational scoops, partly political,
Bold banner headlines, sometimes satirical.

Stringers, hacks, freelance reporters,
Bringing good news to Rotherham supporters.

For editorials with outspoken views,
There's *The Independent* and *Milton Keynes News*.

To circulate news like church bell chimes,
It's *The Kingston, Surbiton and New Malden Times*.

For news reports that are blunt and candid,
There's the *News of the World* and *The Southend Standard*.

The catchy titles that win the champagne
Are *The Penwith Pirate* and *Caerphilly Campaign*.

But when browsing through shelves, what would you make,
Of a sheet with the masthead *The Banbury Cake?*

And for those in Ilkley, with places to let,
There's only one voice: *The Ilkley Gazette*.

For trustworthy news for the Scottish nation,
*The Scotsman* is their own publication.

For licentious pictures and news of a sort,
The sheet for you is *The Daily Sport*.

For easy reading, let's say at a bar,
There's *The Sun, The Globe* or the *Swindon Star*.

Sharp investors and the discerning reader,
Buy the *FT* and the *Mid-Sussex Leader*.

They disseminate news like a raging fire,
*The Mirror, The Telegraph* and *West Craven Town Crier*.

Personally speaking, as a perpetual worrier,
I read *The Guardian* and *The Ramsey Courier*.

I recommend, for those with the stamina,
*The Sunday Observer* or the *Manx Examiner*.

*Y Pentan* for news of the Celtic Kernal,
Like the *South Wales Argus* and *Derry Journal*.

Who waves the flag with banner unfurled?
*The Daily Express* and the *Widnes World*.

But some do say, for journalism without peer,
It's the *Craven Herald and Pioneer*.

There are others who say they don't come better,
Than the *Mail*, the *Post* and the *Belfast Newsletter*.

Leading the field of investigative probe,
Are *The Times, The Shuttle* and *The Wirral Globe*.

For me, the peak nostalgic dekko,
Is *The Liverpool* or *The Dorset Echo*.

To titles long gone we should build a memorial,
For *The Sketch, The Graphic* and *The Sunday Pictorial*.

I feel that it's time to end this address,
So Ladies and Gentlemen, I give you – the Press!

March '06

# MAP READING

The images they conjure, rural, feudal, thatch and snow,
These place-names of old England, Lytchett Minster, Westward Ho!
Some are geographical, telling roughly where they lie,
Named before the post, I sometimes wonder why.
I shall list a few examples that have a strange appeal,
You may sense the isolation and a slightly eerie feel.

Like that old wireless favourite, "Much Binding in the Marsh",
They can describe a landscape, often fairly harsh:

> Hinton in the Hedges
> St Mary in the Marsh
> Widecombe in the Moor

And again

> Gringley on the Hill
> Woughton on the Green
> Waltham on the Wolds

Some, unsure of their actual space,
Prefer to add a second place:

> Weston by Welland
> Sturton by Stour
> Normanby by Spital

Like those who stagger from a bar,
Some are unsure of where they are;

> Stow cum Quy
> Salcott cum Virley
> Hockwold cum Wilton

Of course, since the conquest in 1066,
Some of the place-names have an Anglo-French mix:

> Hutton le Hole
> Kimond le Mire
> Whittle le Wood

## POETRY SEMI-SKIMMED

Living 'on' I can understand, but living under?
Were they living in caves? You have to wonder:

> Milton under Wychwood
> Weston under Lizard
> Wotton under Edge

Is there, just maybe, a hint of a boast,
In announcing their village is on the coast?

> Shoreham by Sea
> Saltburn by the Sea
> Wells next the Sea

"Super", did they mean above, beyond, over, higher,
Or surpassing all others? If the latter, it's dire:

> Peterston super Ely
> St Bride's super Netherwent
> Weston super Mare

Yet others have voted against solitude
To a second place they're now firmly glued:

> Huyton with Roby
> Newton with Scoles
> North Leverton with Hobblesthorpe

Putting these geographical descriptions aside,
Countless others act as historical guides.

Behind each place-name lies an interesting tale,
Embellished in the local by a few pints of ale
And to all these wonderful places, like Moreton on the Lugg,
I shall raise my glass in my sacred space, Boozing in the Snug.

August '06

# THE FAMOUS FIVE RING THEIR RED KITE

The Famous Five, alert and alive,
Set out to ring their Red Kite.
Then slithered, slipped and over they tipped,
In the wood, by the evening light.

Who led the way? Why courageous BJ,
In front of his sister Mali,
Known to us as the Flower of Ty Mawr,
Across the bridge, in the valley.

Then came the three who are known to me,
As the talented trio from Pandy
When Anest the Blest almost went West,
As she fell in wild garlic – grandly.

Siwan and Leusa, somewhat wiser,
Followed the leader in line,
The smell where they fell, in bluebell dell,
Was almost like a sweet wine.

## POETRY SEMI-SKIMMED

As the only "him", young Benjamin,
Hacked out a path to the tree
Then gave the sign at an enormous pine,
Whose top they could hardly see.

The nest held wings and other things,
For some to keep in their hats.
As the Famous Five were eaten alive,
By a million trillion gnats.

But let's be fair, there were others there,
Following on in line,
With ladders, hopes and long, long ropes,
And a man to climb the pine.

"There's half a lamb and a tin of Spam!"
He shouted down from the nest,
"And one little chick with feathers quite thick."
The hen, and them, had been blest.

It bumped and jumped in its muslin bag,
Descending the totem tree.
Debagged and tagged, measured and treasured,
Then raised again to be free.

To show contempt at the way things went,
It soaked the tagger in poo.
Hen and chick must have laughed themselves sick,
They knew it would set like glue.

A rude noise was heard – and not from the bird,
The Five looked as one towards Gwenda
Then the man who broke wind admitted he'd sinned
And Sian asked if a tune he could render.

The Five, almost whacked, then homeward tracked,
With another memory to store,
For every child should see kites in the wild,
It's something they'll 'see' evermore.

But it's thanks to their granddad, Taid Hafnant,
That their big adventure took place,
He helps them to know that the older they grow,
All life is entitled to space.

June '03

# LANCIA

On October 11$^{th}$ 1998, the following appeal appeared in the *Sunday Citizen* (Milton Keynes):

> 1952 Aston Martin lady from Leeds, body 5' 6"
> long, blonde roof, blue headlights, seeking a
> 1938-1952 Ferrari man that is still firing on
> all cylinders, for cruising and posing in the
> Milton Keynes area. Call….

## POETRY SEMI-SKIMMED

As any personnel department will tell you, if you use kinky adverts you get kinky applicants. My reply follows:

Dear 1952 Model Lady from Leeds
(Or may I call you Lancia?)

I note your appeal for a 1938-1952 range Ferrari man in this week's *Sunday Citizen*. As an alternative worthy of consideration, may I offer my 1936 British bull-nosed Morris? Yes, the Italian stable does offer passion and panache, ideal vehicles in which to achieve your glitzy short term aims, but I do urge you to consider a LTR. As a 1952 model, your sump may be showing signs of silting, in which case you may see the advantages of a slower, steady, long-haul relationship, for which I do recommend the steadfast qualities of my 1936 bull-nosed Morris.

The body, though never deemed worthy of public display, is holding up remarkably well, the result of sixty-two years of diligent maintenance by its one owner, the record of which is available. In today's rush into STRs, negative points are hidden and remain unseen until too late; in a display of openness (part of Morris' yesteryear values) I list the negatives as follows:

Rust spots are beginning to appear.
The exhaust is blowing.
Overheating is a frequent problem.
A small but steady coolant leak persists.
Radiator hoses are clogging up.
One cylinder has ceased firing, resulting in a loss

of Power. This, along with the prohibitive expense of replacement parts, has reduced outings to the occasional fine weekend; demanding drives are best avoided.
The starting handle requires two hands to fire the engine. A faulty ventilation system ensures a misting up of the interior, reducing visibility considerably.

Modesty (more old-world charm) forbids a list of positives, except to say that what a Morris lacks in passion, it makes up with a GSOH (essential with a Morris), the willingness to share pleasure and a deep sense of belonging. In anticipation of your acceptance of this offer, I am having my bull-nose chromed.

Yours, in any gear,
Austin Morris                                                    Oct 1998

*LTR: Long term relationship.*
*STR: Short term relationship,*
*GSOH: Good sense of humour.*

Did I send this reply? No, of all the luck, that very week my big ends went; besides, I don't think she was an Aston Martin lady, I think she was from an Escort agency.

# EPILOGUE

Dear Reader

With 'Fear and Trepidation',
I laid these poems before you,
Criticise them if you must,
But be gentle I implore you,
And think on, what often makes a poem compelling,
Lies not in the mind, but in the telling.

www.ingramcontent.com/pod-product-compliance
Lightning Source LLC
Chambersburg PA
CBHW061330040426
42444CB00011B/2856